COVENANT BIBLE STUDIES

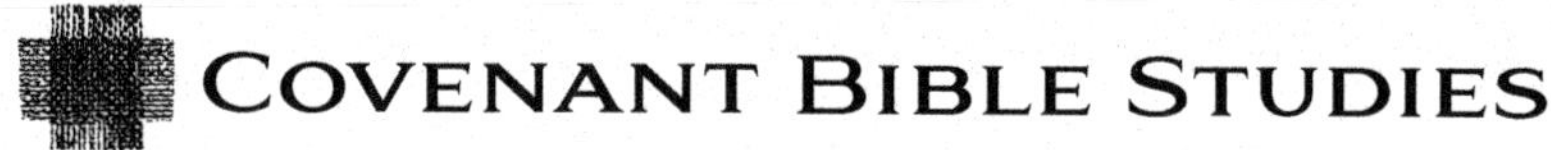

Sabbath: God's Call to Peace

Angela Finet

For a list of Covenant Bible Studies,
visit www.brethrenpress.com.

Sabbath: God's Call to Peace
Covenant Bible Studies Series

Library of Congress Control Number: 2025002851

ISBN 978-0-87178-376-9

Manufactured in the United States of America

Contents

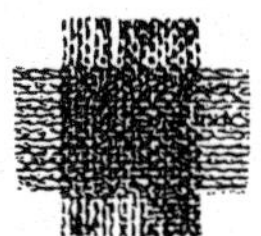

Foreword

What does it mean to live a life of integrity and authenticity? What does the Bible say about the challenges we face at home, in the workplace, in our neighborhoods and communities? How does Christian faith inform the choices we make every day?

The Covenant Bible Studies series seeks to help participants find answers to these and other questions about living as faithful Christians in our world today. Each study encourages small groups to reflect, pray, and learn together.

Covenant Bible Studies are anchored in covenantal history. God covenanted with people in the Old Testament, established a new covenant in Jesus Christ, and through the presence of the Holy Spirit covenants with the church today. Thus, this Bible study is intended for small groups of people who can meet on a regular basis, gathering around God's word to discern its meaning for today, and share openly with one another.

An atmosphere of trust is built within the group, in which support will grow and faith will deepen. Each person's contribution is needed and valued. As each one contributes to study and prayer, the group becomes the real body of Christ. "For just as the body is one and has many members, and all the members of the body, though many, are one body, so it is with Christ" (1 Cor. 12:12).

Each chapter in this Covenant Bible Study is made up of four parts:

- *Prepare*—reading, studying, and reflecting on the material beforehand
- *Share and Pray*—fostering intimacy through personal sharing and prayer
- *Study*—exploring the Bible lesson together
- *Discuss and Act*—digging deeper into the biblical text, discovering its meaning for today, and preparing to go out again into the world

Welcome to this study. As you search the scriptures, may God's voice and guidance and the love and encouragement of brothers and sisters in Christ challenge you to live more fully the abundant life God promises.

Preface

When we hear the word "sabbath," it probably conjures up First Testament images of God resting on the seventh day of creation and commanding the wandering Israelites to "remember the Sabbath and keep it holy." Perhaps we have an inkling of all the rules that surround the observation of the Sabbath, and it feels overwhelming or archaic.

If we think about sabbath in the Second Testament, it likely brings to mind the many times the Pharisees and Scribes set out to trap Jesus for healing or harvesting on the Sabbath, causing us to wonder: Is that all sabbath is for—an opportunity to shout "gotcha!" at our neighbors? Is there anything of benefit to us today in practicing sabbath?

While Jesus didn't command those who followed him to practice all the laws surrounding the Sabbath, he certainly modeled sabbath behavior. He was often in the synagogue with the gathered faith community on the Sabbath. And time after time, Scripture tells us that Jesus preached and healed and cast out demons—Jesus worked—and then withdrew to a deserted place to commune with God, to honor the Sabbath.

We live in a world that is increasingly less mindful of the need for sabbath. We are often judged, and even self-assessed, by our productivity, and sabbath-keeping is viewed as mere laziness. Author Wayne Muller suggests that what modern society would consider a successful life is actually a violent enterprise, saying that we make war on our bodies, our children, our spirit, our communities, and the earth by our unwillingness to make time for gentle tending to them.

Disregarding sabbath practices doesn't just affect our mental, physical, and spiritual health, it also affects the communities in which we live, work, worship, and serve. Muller says it "dictates the way we respond to suffering and it shapes the ways in which we seek peace and healing in the world" (3).

In his book *Conjectures of a Guilty Bystander*, Thomas Merton agreed.

> There is a pervasive form of contemporary violence to which the idealist most easily succumbs: activism and overwork. The rush and pressure of modern life are a form, perhaps the most common form, of its innate violence. To allow oneself to be carried away by a multitude of conflicting concerns, to surrender to too many demands, to commit oneself to too many projects, to want to help everyone in everything, is to succumb to violence. The frenzy of our activism neutralizes our work for peace. It destroys our own inner capacity for peace" (as quoted in Muller, 3).

As people of peace, we understand that God's shalom is more than the absence of violence. In the same way, sabbath is much more than the absence of work. In this study, we will expand our understanding of *Sabbath* as *God's Call to Peace*—peace with God, creation, and neighbor; peace of God, Jesus, and creation; and peace as freedom and justice for all. We will explore together how intentional acts of sabbath-keeping benefit not only self, but society as well.

In a world that is addicted to overwork and exhaustion, this Bible study invites us into a new (and yet ancient) way of living: peacefully, simply, together. As Rabbi Abraham Heschel puts it, "The seventh day [Sabbath] is the armistice in humanity's cruel struggle for existence, a truce in all conflicts, personal and social, peace between person and person, humankind and nature, peace within each one" (29).

It is my prayer that, in spending set-apart time with God and neighbor as you work through this book, you will experience the outlandish peace that sabbath has to offer. May it become the rhythm of your life.

Angela Finet
Mount Wolf, Pennsylvania

1. Sabbath as Restorative Peace

Genesis 1:1–2:3; Hebrews 4:1-11

Prepare

1. Sit in a comfortable position. Close your eyes and relax. Notice the rhythm of your breath. On your inhale, pray, "God's call is peace." On your exhale, pray, "I am at rest." Repeat this exercise for at least one minute.
2. In both Jewish and Christian traditions, the lighting of a candle marks the beginning of the observance of the Sabbath. Light a candle. Wave your hands across the top of the flame as a gesture of bringing sabbath's peace into your space, and into your heart.
3. Read the Genesis passage. In a journal, make note of the words and phrases that are repeated throughout the passage. Do you notice a rhythm unfolding?

Share and Pray

1. Ensure that each person in the group is welcomed with the invitation to share their name and, for fun, the day of the week they were born (easily found on the Internet).

2. Enter into a time of rhythmic, responsive prayer. As each person shares their concern or praise, the group will respond: "In your hearing, in your presence, hear our prayer for peace." Share a moment of silence for unspoken prayers, then conclude with the shared, spoken response.

3. Describe a time when you were keenly aware of the presence of God. Where were you? Did it seem as though time stood still? What did you see, hear, smell, or feel that revealed God's company in your midst? What emotions lingered long after the awareness of the encounter?

4. What is the rhythm of your day? Do you have a scheduled appointment to spend time with God? Describe your daily sabbath habits to the group.

5. Do you set aside a day for sabbath weekly? What does the day include? If this is your habit, how does it feel when you miss a day? If this is not your habit, what prevents you from practicing a weekly sabbath rest? Are there small steps you could take to make weekly sabbath a reality?

6. In her poem "A Postcolonial Tale," poet Joy Harjo writes: "Every day is a reenactment of the creation story. We emerge from dense unspeakable material, through the shimmering power of dreaming stuff." How might these words invite you into a rhythm of renewal each day?

It might seem as if this study could have skipped the first chapter of Genesis and gone straight to chapter 2, the seventh day. After all, this story is familiar, it's long, and the topic we wish to discuss seemingly isn't mentioned in those first thirty-one verses.

But if we had done that, we would have missed the point and poetry of the story: the rhythm of creation. This story demonstrates the God-given *rhythm* of all created things.

The Rhythm of Sabbath

I love the rhythmic flow of this Genesis passage. I can feel my body gently sway as though I'm on a boat, or a hammock, as the words tickle my ears. You can hear it in the repetition that God created, took stock, and declared it good.

Created
Saw
Declared it good.

It's like a heartbeat. Like a breath.

I love the rhythmic flow of this Genesis passage. I can feel my body gently sway as though I'm on a boat, or a hammock, as the words tickle my ears. You can hear it in the repetition that God created, took stock, and declared it good.

This passage tells us that the creative process has a rhythm. God spoke, and it was so. And the days had a rhythm. You see, this story is all about rhythm, not about 24-hour units of time. There was evening. There was morning. The first day.

Think about that rhythm for just a second. Notice the order.

There was evening. There was morning. The first day. We think the day begins at the crack of dawn when the rooster crows. But that's not how scripture describes it at all.

In her book *Liturgy of the Ordinary: Sacred Practices in Everyday Life*, Tish Harrison Warren offers insight regarding the evening/morning rhythm: "In Jewish culture, days begin in the evening with the setting of the sun. . . . The day begins with rest. We start [our day] by settling down and going to sleep. This understanding of time is powerfully reorienting, even jarring, to those of us who measure our days by our own efforts and accomplishments. The Jewish day begins in seemingly accomplishing nothing at all. We begin by resting, drooling on our pillow, dropping off into helplessness" (150). Harrison emphasizes that the day *begins* with rest.

Everything in scripture that follows from this Genesis passage contains a rhythm of rest:

Rest each day.
Rest on the seventh day.
Rest in the seventh year.
Rest in the fiftieth year—the Jubilee.

On the Seventh Day God Created

We hear the daily rhythm in chapter 1. But then we get to chapter 2, the seventh day. On the seventh day, God *created* rest. Sabbath is part of the created order.

Read Genesis 2:3 again, this time from *The Voice* paraphrase: "Thus, God blessed day seven and made it special—*an open time for pause and restoration, a sacred zone of Sabbath-keeping*, because God rested from all the work He had done in creation that day."

Do you notice the hint that God is still creating? Even on day seven?

Ancient rabbinical tradition teaches that God did not finish the work of creation—the heavens and earth and the multitudes—until the seventh day.

Author Wayne Muller writes: "The ancient rabbis teach that on the seventh day, God created *menuha*—which means tranquility, serenity, peace, and repose. In other words, God created rest, in the deepest possible sense of fertile, healing stillness. Until the Sabbath, creation was unfinished. Only after the birth of menuha, only with tranquility and rest, was the circle of creation made full and complete" (37).

***Menuha* means so much more than simply ceasing from labor and exertion. It offers so much more than freedom from toil, strain, or activity of any kind. *Menuha* is not a "thou shalt not" but a "thou shalt." As one made in the image of the One who rests, *thou shalt* also rest. *Thou shalt* lean into the rhythm of creation—in the presence of the Creator.**

What makes the practice of sabbath different from rest? I believe the difference is *menuha*. *Menuha* means so much more than simply ceasing from labor and exertion. It offers so much more than freedom from toil, strain, or activity of any kind. *Menuha* is not a "thou shalt not," but rather a "thou shalt." As one made in the image of the One who rests, *thou shalt* also rest. *Thou shalt* lean into the rhythm of creation—in the presence of the Creator.

The Gift of Sabbath

In her book *Flunking Sainthood*, Jana Riess explores Rabbi Abraham Joshua Heschel's book *The Sabbath*. She explores his approach to space and time and how we spend our lives.

> Most of life, he says, is a struggle to conquer the space around us: we conquer space when we pay our mortgage, battle any kudzu that threatens to encroach in the yard, or venture forth from our homes to wage the incessant war that is earning a living. But it's a tradeoff. We can only conquer that space, he explains, when we sacrifice time.

> And after some years of this, a surprising thing happens: we come to dread blank time without that war of busyness, because here we have to face the truth of who we are and what we're doing (83).

When, through our practice of sabbath, we imitate the God who rested, we are reminded of who we are: people made in God's image. When we practice sabbath, we become more aware of God's presence.

And here we really get to the heart of it all. "Sabbath is the presence of God in the world, open to the soul of man. God is not in things of space, but in moments of time" (Heschel xiv).

Later, in Exodus, we find that observing the Sabbath is part of the Ten Commandments—part of the covenant between God and Israel. But here, in the beginning, sabbath is part of creation—a gift for *all* people, and for every created thing.

Heschel writes, "The Sabbath is the most precious present mankind has received from the treasure house of God. All week we think: The spirit is too far away, and we succumb to spiritual absenteeism, or at best we pray: Send us a little of Thy spirit. On the Sabbath the spirit stands and pleads: accept all excellence from me" (18).

Sabbath is one of God's very first gifts to God's beloved creation. Not simply a gift of rest, but a gift of time . . . a gift of presence. A gift that restores peace to our bodies, minds, and souls.

And it's a gift we're often not inclined to receive. That's not a new story either. We find it again in Hebrews 4:9-11: "So then, a Sabbath rest still remains for the people of God, for those who enter God's rest also rest from their labors as God did from his. Let us therefore make every effort to enter that rest, so that no one may fall through such disobedience as theirs."

Disobeying, or refusing this gift of God's rest, leads to violence—to self, to family, to community, to creation. It leads to destruction rather than restoration.

Resting on the Sabbath is a witness to peace. It's a sign that God's creative order continues to exist in the present. When all the world rests on the Sabbath, it demonstrates that all are in right relationship with the Creator, and God's created order will once again be complete; be restored; be realized as it was in the beginning.

Resting on the Sabbath is a witness to peace. It's a sign that God's creative order continues to exist in the present. When all the world rests on the Sabbath, it demonstrates that all are in right relationship with the Creator, and God's created order will once again be complete; be restored; be realized as it was in the beginning.

In their daily practice of sabbath, our Jewish brothers and sisters include in their evening prayers a petition based on a promise found in Psalm 121, that God will guard their going out and coming in.

But on the seventh-day Sabbath, the prayer is different. Instead of requesting protection from harm, it declares that God will embrace us with a tent of peace.

Discuss and Act

1. Is there a difference between sabbath and rest? If so, how would you describe it?
2. Look up the words to verse 2 in the hymn "Great Is Thy Faithfulness." Note that "strength for today and bright hope for tomorrow" flows from reflecting on God's creation. In the Genesis passage, the text begins with chaos, becomes orderly due to God's creative work, and results in peaceful rest. How might remembering God's creative power to bring structure from a swirling mess encourage you and give you peace when life is challenging?
3. In Genesis 1:31, God saw everything that God had made and named it very good. Considering this verse, it's clear God rested not out of exhaustion, but out of satisfaction for work well done. How might reflecting on this verse invite us to spend our sabbath time delighting in the work we have completed rather than worrying about all the work yet left to do?
4. How might you bring a moment of sabbath to someone in the midst of their busy, chaotic, or physically intense workday?
5. God invites us to imitate God in creative endeavors and has prepared work in advance for us to do. On the Sabbath, how might we respond to the reminder that six days a week, we work and create, but on the seventh day, we rest as a part of creation?
6. The Hebrews text speaks to a rest that was, and is, and is yet to come. How do you experience and anticipate God's rest?

2. Sabbath as Peace with God

Exodus 20:1-17; Colossians 3:5; John 15:1-8; Psalm 46:10

Prepare

1. Sit in a comfortable position. Relax your shoulders and take several deep breaths. As you inhale, pray the words, "Abide in me." As you exhale fully, pray the words, "As I abide in you." Repeat this practice for as long as you need.
2. Read the words to the hymn "Abide with Me." How do these words reflect the practice of sabbath peace? Write down the words and images that feel especially meaningful today.
3. Read the Ten Commandments, found in Exodus 20:1-17. Instead of a series of "Thou shall nots," try reframing them in a positive way. For instance, one could rewrite verse 16, "You shall not bear false witness against your neighbor," to say, "You must speak truthfully to people so that walls of deceit are not built between you and them."

Share and Pray

1. Greet one another by sharing your name and five words to describe yourself. For example, you could say you are a birdwatcher, mother, bargain-shopper, Christian, schoolteacher. Now rank them in order

of how much time you spend actively participating in each of these roles, from most to least. Given the opportunity, would you like to reorder any of the items on your list? Why?

2. Share your burdens and blessings from the week. Once everyone who wishes has shared, say the following prayer together: "Thank you for your presence, God. You are with us in this space, and you are in the midst of each situation we've shared. Your loving presence fills us with peace. Amen."

3. Read together the Ten Commandments, found in Exodus 20:1-17. Share the ways you rewrote them in Prepare no. 3. Focus especially on the first two commandments found in verses 3-6. How does hearing them phrased in a different way enhance your understanding?

4. The word "idolatry" is described in the *Oxford Dictionary Online* as the worship of false gods. How would you define the practice of idolatry? Read Colossians 3:5. How does that verse definite idolatry?

5. Consider what idols you have allowed to take the place of your time spent with God. As you pray together, ask God to show you where you are (mis)placing your trust. Ask for God's help to prune those things away and give you peace.

How does the passage from Exodus relate to the passage from the Gospel of John? At first glance, you might think, "not at all." But actually, the Ten Commandments and the Farewell Discourse (where this passage from John resides) are focused on the creation of a *people*. And they both provide instructions for how that newly formed community is to function.

The Exodus passage is the first time recorded in Scripture that God speaks to the gathered community of Israel, and the John passage records the last time Jesus speaks to the assembled disciples prior to his death and resurrection.

The Exodus passage is the first time recorded in Scripture that God speaks to the gathered community of Israel, and the John passage records the last time Jesus speaks to the assembled disciples prior to his death and resurrection. These passages are very different in style, but they have a lot in common. Both passages begin with "I am" statements. And both passages call the people to peace with their God.

God's Call to Relationship

The introduction to the Ten Commandments hints that this is more than just a series of rules. This is God's revelation, from God's own mouth, of who God is—the God of liberation and freedom. These commandments provide the framework for a covenantal relationship with this liberating God!

In a covenantal relationship, there must be faithfulness, fidelity, and allegiance born out of love, not fear-mongering, dominance, and control. The beauty is that this covenant, by definition, is not one-way. God is not asking us for something that God isn't willing to offer in return. This first command reminds us that nothing should interfere with our relationship with God. Nothing should be allowed to take God's place in our lives.

God knows us and knows how easily we are distracted and enticed to give in to the norms of our society where competition rules, and productivity and accumulation is celebrated. We often respond to the still small voice that whispers, "What harm can there be in checking your email . . . constantly?" instead of the One who says, "Be still, and know that I am God!"

Time after time, we neglect our first love. Yet, God still calls us to a peaceful existence that comes from placing our trust in God and letting go of those things that slowly drain the lifeforce out of us.

What Is My Idol?

It is appropriate to spend some time with this question. We may be tempted to play the ancient game of "but who is my neighbor?" by suggesting that we don't have any idols! After all, there isn't a single graven image in our homes!

But anything can become an idol when we seek from it the kind of peace and security that only God can provide. In fact, our self-sufficiency may be our

Anything can become an idol when we seek from it the kind of peace and security that only God can provide. In fact, our self-sufficiency may be our biggest idol of all! Thankfully, God provides a remedy, reminding us that idols lose their grip on us when we put them in their proper place—below God.

biggest idol of all! Thankfully, God provides a remedy, reminding us that idols lose their grip on us when we put them in their proper place—below God.

God's second command expands on this idea. We create false gods by putting other things before God, and sometimes those idols we've created become visual, tangible things taking up space in our lives. We don't need an image of God's presence . . . we need God's *actual* presence. An image doesn't take the place of a relationship.

It's interesting that, as God walked with Adam and Eve in the garden, there is no description of God's appearance. But there is language of the "image of God" —and it is in the people themselves. People were created in the image of God, so perhaps one way we experience God is in the presence of God's image—God's people. Are we reflecting the image of God to one another?

As we spend time with God, we grow ever more into God's likeness, and the things we desire align ever more with God's desires. We become people of God's peace.

Abide with Me

Sometimes I imagine what I would say to my beloveds if I knew it were my last night on earth. I would want my words to be inspiring and important, and to point them in the way they should continue on without me. I would keep it simple, and repeat it over and over.

In his Farewell Discourse in John 15, Jesus employs these tactics. In just eight verses, Jesus uses the word "abide" eight times. Perhaps we should take note. Jesus instructs us to continue his work, but not without first abiding.

He instructs that we are not as useful or as productive as we think we are if we're severed from the source of inspiration—the source of life. Paradoxically, perhaps, more abiding produces more fruit, not less. We are told to bear fruit—but not at the expense of our relationship with Jesus.

In fact, branches that bend to the idol of productivity are only useful as wood for the fire. When you consider Jesus' statement in that light, it sounds less like a punishment than an apt description. Jesus says these branches are entirely consumed. Perhaps that's where we get the notion of "burnout."

In her book *Sacred Rest,* Saundra Dalton-Smith described this very experience in her life. In a moment of extreme exhaustion, she found herself on her back on the floor. When her husband asked what she was doing, her answer was "burning." She described her productivity-induced fatigue as feeling like kindling being fully consumed by a fire (4-5).

When we are burned out, we are living a fruitless life. Lack of attention to our physical, emotional, and spiritual need for rest drains our lives of hope and joy, even though we may appear to be quite productive and successful.

The best grapes, the ones that are sweetest and plumpest, are formed closest to the vine. This is why branches are pruned and kept short. By abiding in Jesus, we are demonstrating our trust in him and his plans. We get into trouble when we put all our trust in our own strength (thereby creating an idol).

The best grapes, the ones that are sweetest and plumpest, are formed closest to the vine. This is why branches are pruned and kept short. By abiding in Jesus, we are demonstrating our trust in him and his plans. We get into trouble when we put all our trust in our own strength (thereby creating an idol).

The society in which we live encourages independence and the idea of pulling ourselves up by our bootstraps. But this is not the way of peace. As God prunes us, it is important to dwell not on what was lost, but on the new, sweet life it fosters.

Do Not Be Afraid

This may require a significant shift in perspective. We may have learned somewhere along the way to fear rest. We may worry that if we don't care for the poor or feed the hungry (or whatever task we feel called to), who will? Often, we care for others with great conviction, but do we care for ourselves with that same sense of call and passion? Jesus says that we must take time to abide with him. Apart from him, we can do nothing.

Sometimes we let fear dictate where we spend our time and resources. We may fear missing out on what others are doing, or fear that resources will not stretch far enough, especially when confronted with the consumerism of our age. In these moments, it is easy to focus on self and our ability to meet our own needs and solve our own problems. Self-reliance is one of our biggest idols, and it does not lead to peace. Into this place of fear, Jesus beckons: "Abide with me."

Discuss and Act

1. How do the phrases "I am the Lord your God" and "I am the true vine" guide you in ordering your priorities? Do both phrases sound like invitations to relationship? Why or why not?

2. What does it mean to bear fruit in a way that glorifies God? How can we draw ourselves back to the vine when we start comparing our "fruit production" to that of others?

3. It takes more than a single grape to provide living sustenance. The very best grape cannot do much without the sweet juice of others. How does this image inform the work we do as a church, as a community working together?

4. Self-sufficiency is considered a virtue today. But how might the practice of self-sufficiency lead to violence against self, family, community, and/or creation? What actions could you take to increase your dependence on God?

5. It is easy to make assumptions about how people choose to spend their time. How might we resist the temptation to judge others, and instead ask if there is a way we could help them make time for sabbath and for relationships? What type of new ministry could emerge through our efforts—one that fosters connection between us and with God?

6. What is your greatest fear about relinquishing control to God? If you're comfortable, share with the group.

3. Sabbath as Peace of God

Exodus 20:8-11; Exodus 31:13; Ephesians 2:1-10

Prepare

1. Find a comfortable position and take three cleansing breaths. Thank God for the things you are noticing in this moment and for God's presence in your daily living. Pray about areas of your life where you need more of God's presence and offer them up to God.

2. Spend a moment in confession, naming ways you participate in the work-with-no-rest culture of this world. This may include having others work to serve you on *their* day of rest. Ask God to bring hidden times into the light and better align you with divine values.

3. Seeking the kingdom of God is not just for the Sabbath day. Try creating a mental sanctuary to which you can retreat throughout each day. For example, choose a characteristic of God—like love, joy, peace, kindness, goodness, gentleness, faithfulness, and so on—and take a few minutes to just focus on that attribute. Write it down if that's helpful. Notice how this practice reduces your stress or anxiety.

Share and Pray

1. Light a candle. Share this traditional Sabbath blessing in unison:

"Blessed are you, God of the Sabbath, who has made us a people through the commandments, and commanded us to kindle the Sabbath lights." Pray silently for God's peace to descend.

2. Share prayer requests with one another. After each person shares, say together, "God, we trust that you are moving. Help us rest in you."

3. As you are comfortable, share a moment this week where you noticed God's peaceful presence. Did your awareness change anything in that moment?

4. Sing or read together the hymn "I Come to the Garden Alone." What images of "tarrying" with God does this song invoke? How might you practice this invitation?

In 2018, a poll was conducted by YouGov, a British market research firm, and Y2 Analytics, an American firm, on behalf of *Deseret News*. The purpose of the poll was to determine whether the Ten Commandments were still relevant today. Interestingly, the American respondents largely claimed some sort of religious affiliation, and 90 percent of them affirmed that the commands against murder, stealing, and lying were essential to healthy, communal living.

However, even with a religious predisposition, fewer than half of the respondents felt God's command to practice sabbath was a necessary component to a flourishing society. In fact, the fourth commandment received the lowest ranking of the ten. We can imagine that a poll conducted among a more secular group of respondents might find even lower support for sabbath rest.

And yet, God's command to honor the Sabbath is the one that God spends the most time explaining. God commands that we spend time, not just in resting, but in preparation for set-apart rest. Sabbath is not intended to be an afterthought—the last-minute cessation of labor when (or if) the workday or work week is done. Sabbath is the starting point: the life-giving rhythm of rest that nurtures peace in our lives.

Honor the Sabbath

Many laws and rules surround the practice of the Sabbath. Why might that be? If you consider the rules broadly, you'll see that they primarily prohibit tasks that women, slaves, and servants would traditionally perform. God makes it clear that everyone is called to a set-apart time to commune with God, because everyone needs to be reminded of their worth solely as one made in the image of God.

I find it interesting that this fourth commandment serves as the lynchpin between the commandments to honor God and those that honor community. Practicing sabbath shapes and centers all our relationships. It commands us to take a full day to luxuriate in God's loving presence and then carry that feeling of being loved into every other encounter and relationship in our lives.

Sabbath is not just a day off. It's a regular reminder that our identity comes from who and whose we *are*, not what we *do*. The fact that we need God's weekly reminder speaks to how easily we succumb to the temptation to find our worth elsewhere. Breaking this commandment, perhaps more than any of the others, harms our ability to live at peace with our Creator, with our neighbor, and even with ourselves.

Breaking this commandment, perhaps more than any others, harms our ability to live at peace with our Creator, with our neighbor, and even with ourselves.

Through God's commandments, we understand God's will for us. God desires that we should have life and have it abundantly. Ignoring God's commands jeopardizes us, not because God is waiting to smite and punish us, but because we suffer when we refuse God's longing to fill us with vibrancy and to give us life.

Conspiring with Empire?

Ephesians 2 tells us that we are dead through sin when we live like the people of this world. Many will tell you this means we are to live morally, with high ethics—basically following commandments five through ten. That is certainly part of the equation.

But the fact that this passage ends with the reminder that there is nothing we can *do* to save our lives suggests there is more to the story. We are reminded that we are made whole not by our actions, but by our faith.

The world, powers, and empires tell us over and over that we must do something to demonstrate our worth. Through hard work, they tell us, we can prove our value. When we act on those lies, we are conspiring with empire. Why would we do that? The empire doesn't care about us!

I wonder why is it so difficult to believe that God loves us and yearns to spend time with us? Why would we say "no" to this incredible offer?

I wonder why is it so difficult to believe that God loves us and yearns to spend time with us? Why would we say "no" to this incredible offer? Is it fear? A lack of trust? Surely, constant striving, fueled by fear, is the opposite of the life of peace to which God calls us.

Is it fear? A lack of trust? Surely, constant striving, fueled by fear, is the opposite of the life of peace to which God calls us.

When we say "yes" to God's offer of sabbath, we operate from a well-rested place, and joyfully do the work God prepared for us. What a different experience that is from taking on the burdens of work laid on us by the powers of the world.

The world's work is always a quid pro quo: we only receive based on effort we put in (and often, we are not compensated fairly). Sabbath is the reminder that God's economy isn't like that of empire. We don't need to work ourselves to death to earn God's affection. We simply enjoy the good works God has put before us as an opportunity to bless others, while we ourselves are also blessed.

When we say "yes" to God's offer of sabbath, we operate from a well-rested place, and joyfully do the work God prepared for us. What a different experience that is from taking on the burdens of work laid on us by the powers of the world.

It's critical to understand that being "dead through sin" doesn't mean we constantly make ethical and moral lapses. It means we continue to live into the conformity of the world—the conformity that includes taking on the values of the world like productivity, self-reliance, and work above all else. Even though we are "good people," we are living in sin when we turn our backs on the shalom God wants for us and for the world. When we do not oppose the oppressive powers in our culture, we are complicit in their abuse.

Sabbath as Witness

In Exodus 31:13 (CEB), God says, "Tell the Israelites: 'Be sure to keep my sabbaths, because the Sabbath is a sign between me and you in every generation so you will know that I am the Lord who makes you holy.'"

When we participate in keeping sabbath, we demonstrate to the world where our trust lies. Author Walter Brueggemann writes: "YHWH is a Sabbath-keeping God, which fact ensures that restfulness and not restlessness is at the center of life. YHWH is a Sabbath-giving God and a Sabbath-commanding God. . . . Sabbath becomes a decisive, concrete, visible way of opting for and aligning with the God of rest" (10).

Surrendering to God's command for sabbath gives us time to examine our allegiances and where we spend our energy. It provides us with space to consider some fundamental questions. Are we committed to economic practices that oppress others and perpetrate injustice? Have we conformed to the world that serves the powerful, and neglects those on the margins, or do we actively witness to God's economy through our practice of sabbath?

Are we practicing our faith peacefully if we refuse God's command to rest because we want to demonstrate how hard we work in service to the Lord without ever surrendering to God's rest? If so, what kind of a witness is that?

In an interview about church life and culture, pastor, professor, and writer Eugene Peterson asserted the importance of sabbath-keeping for pastors: "If you don't take Sabbath, something is wrong. You're doing too much. You're being too much in charge. You've got to quit, one day a week, and just watch what God is doing when you're not doing anything."

May it be so, for all of us.

Discuss and Act

1. Having worked through this lesson, are you more aware of a tendency toward self-sufficiency in yourself? If so, how might beginning each morning with the questions, "Where am I putting my allegiance?" and "In whom do I put my trust?" help you focus on the work God is asking you to do?
2. Do you find yourself making lists of the things you need to accomplish before you have *earned* a rest? Do you ever judge whether others have worked hard enough to *earn* a rest? How might things change if you asked instead, "Have I *rested* enough to do the work to which I have been called?" As you are comfortable, share with the group.
3. Ephesians 2:1-2 says that we are dead through our transgressions when we follow the ways of the world. How might it change your perspective on this verse when you consider that the ways of our western

civilization are an unhealthy focus on productivity and making money? Can you envision how that focus leads to "death"?

4. Name other scriptures where Jesus instructs against worry, greed, and the love of money. In light of what you're learning about sabbath, do those stories feel more urgent, poignant, or connected? If so, how?

5. How might you be vocal about the need for sabbath—for yourself and for others? What kind of witness would that be? Are you afraid that others might judge you for taking a radical stance? How might you overcome that fear?

4.

Sabbath as Peace of Creation

Psalm 23; Exodus 20:24, 31:17; 1 Samuel 30:9-10; Psalm 110:7; Matthew 14:13, 22-23

Prepare

1. Find a quiet place to step outside. Lift your shoulders and take a deep breath in, then relax your shoulders and slowly exhale. Continue to breathe and notice your feet pressing into the ground. Meditate for a moment on how the ground is holding you up.
2. Continue breathing and listen for the sounds of nature—rustling leaves, chirping birds, or perhaps the trickle of water. Remember that God breathed creation into being. As you listen, imagine you are hearing the sound of God's breath . . . and align your breathing with God's. How might this vision encourage you to breathe in times of anxiety?
3. Read Psalm 23. Consider the place God leads you to when you're in need of peace, rest, or nourishment for your soul. Rewrite the psalm to describe your experience of God's gentle leading to your place of peace.

Share and Pray

1. Welcome one another with a handshake of peace.

2. Share together your burdens and beauties from the week.
3. In a basin, place a small glass vase or a drinking glass. From two full pitchers of water, slowly fill the glass and watch as it overflows into the basin. As you listen to the trickling water, offer your silent prayers over the needs shared with the group. Finish this time of prayer by saying in unison: "Pour your peace over us. Fill us to overflowing. Restore our souls. Amen."
4. Where do you best see God's miracles? What experiences evoke a sense of gratitude in your life? What helps you hear from God? Share your answers together.
5. Picture your place of peace from Prepare no. 3. Is it near water? Under a canopy of trees? Among blooming flowers where hummingbirds and butterflies flit and fly? The desert? Somewhere else? As you are comfortable, describe your place of peace to one another.
6. Listen to the hymn "Come to the Water" by John Foley. How does this invitation lead you into a posture of prayer?

Read again these familiar words from Psalm 23:2-3: God makes me lie down in green pastures; leads me beside still waters; and restores my soul.

Come to the Water

In the first chapter of Genesis, in the beginning, God spoke creation out of the waters. "The waters" are the birthplace of creation. "The waters" are the birthplace of our formation, too. Maybe somewhere in our subconscious the waters recall to us the safety and protection of our mother's womb.

In the process of writing this study, I asked many people to share their vision of a place of peace. Nearly 80 percent of the time, the answer was "somewhere near the water." That seems like a noteworthy amount. Perhaps the reason for such overwhelming consensus is simply because God leads us there.

In the first chapter of Genesis, in the beginning, God spoke creation out of the waters. "The waters" are the birthplace of creation. "The waters" are the birthplace of our formation, too. Maybe somewhere in our subconscious the waters recall to us the safety and protection of our mother's womb. Maybe that's why water restores our souls. It is a place of birth and rebirth.

A creation story is told in Genesis 1. Chapter 2 picks up with the seventh day—the day God *created* rest. The day God rested. Exodus 31:17 amplifies the story a bit, saying, "in six days the LORD made heaven and earth, and on the seventh day God rested and was refreshed."

This word, "refreshed," literally means that God exhaled. Isn't that beautiful? Again, we sense the rhythm of creation—a life-giving rhythm we can see and hear and feel in our breathing as we inhale and exhale. A rhythm we can see and hear and feel in creation, through the turning of the seasons, the lapping of the gentle waves, the gurgle of the softly flowing brook.

The psalmist says God leads us to these still waters which, translated from the Hebrew *mee menuchoth,* means waters of rest or refreshment. These are quiet and gentle streams—the antidote to the violent rush of great rivers whose turbulence frightens the sheep and threatens to carry them away if they were to stoop to drink. These softly flowing streams are the opposite of the deafening rapids and overwhelming floods of the noisy world. They restore our souls.

David's Men Are Restored

In 1 Samuel 30, we hear an odd story about King David and his army of six hundred men. They had returned from battle only to find that their village had been raided by the Amalekites, who had burned it completely to the ground and taken all of the Israelites' wives, sons, and daughters captive.

After seeking God's guidance, David and his men set out to save their loved ones. You can imagine that every single man wanted to see this rescue mission through. You just know that everyone would have wanted to contribute to the goal of bringing their loved ones home.

But bodies need rest. We have limits. It was at Brook Besor, a shallow ravine, where the men stopped to take a break, only to find that a third of them couldn't continue. They were simply too exhausted to cross even this modest stream. David and the four hundred who were able to carry on left them behind. To rest. To be refreshed. To be restored beside the water.

Once the mission proved successful, David, his men, and all the rescued women and children returned, along with the spoils of victory. And the two hundred men, the ones left behind, were restored—not only to physical and mental health, but to the community.

You see, the four hundred who accompanied David grumbled, not wanting to share the fruits of their labor. But David put their complaining to bed, saying it was God who provided victory, and God who also provided rest—for the healing and wholeness of all.

We worship a God who works and who rests. And we follow a God who is restored at the water.

We worship a God who works and who rests. And we follow a God who is restored at the water.

Consider Psalm 110. This psalm describes God's faithful protection and provision. It pronounces God's judgement on the nations. And it ends with the image of God finding rest and restoration. Drinking from the stream by the path. Demonstrating peace at last.

Or consider Jesus' own practices of pursing peaceful rest. Where did he find healing for his own weary body and mind? Where did he go to commune with God?

Jesus Finds Rest

In Matthew 14, Jesus learned that his beloved cousin, John the Baptist, had been beheaded by King Herod. This is the kind of news that takes your breath away and deeply wounds you in spirit and soul.

Jesus needed a place to restore his mind and spirit from that violent imagery. In verse 13, we learn that his place of peace and renewal was on a boat, surrounded by water that is so often a source of healing miracles. After stepping off the boat, Jesus meets and feeds the hungry crowds who had been following after him, crowds he couldn't have ministered to with a depleted spirit.

Author Wayne Muller writes, "The invitation to rest is rooted in an undeniable spiritual gravity that allows all things at rest to settle, to find their place. There comes a moment in our striving when more effort actually becomes counterproductive, when our frantic busyness only muddies the waters of our wisdom and understanding. When we become still and allow our life to rest, we feel a renewal of energy and gradual clarity of perception" (26).

Jesus prayed and rested on the water. And then he ministered and served.

After feeding the crowd of five thousand, Jesus once again listened to the needs of his own heart and soul and sought another place and time for respite. Matthew 14:22-23 tells us he found communion with God up the mountain where he went to pray.

A faithful translation of the phrase "to pray" is "to come to rest." As Jesus prayed, his body and mind were at rest. He found nourishment and restoration in God's spirit that seems to saturate peaceful places. Sometimes, our prayers take the form of words. Other times, prayer is simply becoming aware of the presence of God as experienced in creation and allowing God's nearness to fill us with peace.

> **We are surrounded by a 24-hour news cycle that blares the worst the world has to offer. God offers, and even commands, an alternative. We need to ask God to lead us to green pastures and not attempt to feed on the world's dry weeds.**

We are surrounded by a 24-hour news cycle that blares the worst the world has to offer. God offers, and even commands, an alternative. We need to ask God to lead us to green pastures rather than attempting to feed on the world's dry weeds.

We need gentle waters to still our souls and to offer peace in this tumultuous and raucous world. We need to find that quiet time and place where we can refocus—a real place of sabbath, a real place of retreat and renewal.

We need to come to the water.

It's not that the water itself is holy. In fact, in every place in scripture where God commands the practice of sabbath, there is no mention of a required place. Indeed, in Exodus 20:24, God says "in *every place* where I cause my name to be remembered I will come to you and bless you" (emphasis added).

And yet, scripture also extends and calls and pleads with us: Come to the water. God *makes* us lie down in green pastures. There is something about God's creation and its rhythms that leads to peace.

Discuss and Act

1. Two hundred of David's men, suffering from exhaustion and in need of renewal, stayed behind at Brook Besor despite the peer pressure to pursue their loved ones' captors. Where are you right now? Are you forging ahead to meet others' expectations, or are you sitting by the brook? If you are comfortable, share your answer.

2. Are there those in your life (family, work colleagues, church members—including pastors) in need of their own Brook Besor moments? How do you respond to them? With judgement, frustration, and shaming? With the offer of rest, but on your time schedule and rhythm? Or with the gift of grace? What might those different responses look like? What results would they produce?

3. I sometimes get my best ideas in the shower. Have you ever had this experience or found other experiences near water that foster deeper connections between you and your Creator? Between your body and mind?

4. In the Matthew passage, Jesus responds to the news of the death of John the Baptist by withdrawing. He does not resort to revenge or violence in kind. How might we emulate Jesus in situations where we might be tempted to react in unhealthy ways? How might we help others respond to tragedy in life-giving ways?

5. The fourth stanza of John Denver's song "Rocky Mountain High" describes his experience of communing with God: "Now he walks in quiet solitude the forest and the streams, Seeking grace in every step he takes, His sight has turned inside himself to try and understand, The serenity of a clear blue mountain lake. . . . You can talk to God and listen to the casual reply." Have you had this experience? If not, how might you make a point to experience God's peace of creation?

6. How might you make an experience with creation possible for neighbors who might need it? Could you sponsor a scholarship for a child to attend summer camp? Or create a community prayer garden on the church property? What specific steps could you take to bring your idea to fruition?

5.

Sabbath as Peace with Creation

Genesis 1:28, 2:15-20; Leviticus 25:1-24; Hosea 4:1-3; Romans 8:18-23

Prepare

1. Take a moment to step outside or sit next to a window on a sunny day. Close your eyes and allow the sun to kiss your skin. Allow God's light to penetrate any darkness you are carrying. Offer thanks for God's mercy.
2. Read the passages from Genesis and Leviticus. Take note of God's intention for creation, paying close attention to the relationship between humans and nature. Write down new insights or understandings.
3. Look out your window or take a walk around your neighborhood. Try to name as many birds, animals, trees, and flowers as you can. For those you can't identify, take pictures and find names for them later.

Share and Pray

1. Welcome one another. Share burdens and blessings of the week, respecting those who wish to pass. Have a volunteer lead in spoken prayer for the items shared. Leave space for silent prayers of the people.

2. Share together things you identified on your nature walk earlier in the week. After each person shares, say together, "Thank you, God, for your creation!"

3. If you had or have pets, share the story of one of their names. Was there a special reason for what you named them? Notice that when you meet someone else's pet, one of the first pieces of information exchanged is the name. Why might that be?

4. Look up the poem "I Go Among Trees" by Wendell Berry. You can find it online, or in his book *A Timbered Choir: The Sabbath Poems 1979-1997*. Read it aloud together. What actions facilitate peace with creation? Have you ever had an experience like this in nature? If you are comfortable, share with the group.

5. Sing, read, or listen to a recording of one of the following hymns: "All Things Bright and Beautiful," "This is My Father's World," or "I Sing the Mighty Power of God." How do these songs describe God's creative power and our response to God's creation?

God does a lot of talking "in the beginning." The words God says are so powerful that simply by speaking them, creation comes into being. In Genesis 1, each of God's creative phrases begins with the word, "let."

However, this rhythm of speech changes in verse 28. This verse records the first time that God speaks *to* a human.

God Names Us Co-Creators

Verse 28 is in the form of a command, but these words are actually an invitation to relationship—not with the Creator, but with creation itself. The command to be fruitful and multiply is an invitation to share in God's creative purposes. God names us co-creators!

God calls us not simply to maintain the earth, but to participate in the creative process. We are partners in helping creation grow in a healthy manner to its fullest potential. After all, God's creation is something that God named "good."

As such, the relationship between humans and creation should mirror the relationship between God and humans. This is a relationship of caretaking and nurturing, not exploitation. God calls us not simply to maintain the earth, but to participate in the creative process. We are partners in helping creation grow in a healthy manner to its fullest potential. After all, God's creation is something that God named "good."

What's in a Name?

We learn more about being God's co-creators in Genesis 2. In this version of the creation story, God instructs humans to name all the birds and animals. Once again, we receive God's invitation to join in God's creative process. In Genesis 1:5, immediately after separating light from darkness, God named them "day" and "night." Naming is part of caring for creation. Biblically speaking, to name something is to bless God for it.

Naming is also part of peacemaking. Did you know that acts of violence almost always begin with hate speech that spirals out of control? This is true on both a personal and a societal scale. The names that we use to identify living things ultimately determine our attitudes, and then our actions, towards them.

For instance, if we begin to belittle another person or group, we start to think of them in terms that diminish their humanity. It then becomes easier to justify our own behavior when we treat them in ways that are unfair or oppressive. Once we have dehumanized others through speech and thought, it's easy to take a next step towards violence. As people of peace, we are called to counteract this violence—and it starts with the names we use!

Once we have dehumanized others through speech and thought, it's easy to take a next step towards violence. As people of peace, we are called to counteract this violence—and it starts with the names we use!

Subdue or Steward?

"The LORD God took the human and settled him in the garden of Eden to farm it and to take care of it" (Genesis 2:15, CEB).

Several English translations of this verse use the word "subdue" to describe God's command regarding humans' care for creation. Once again, word choice matters. Over time, the word "subdue" has seemingly provided permission for abusive and controlling actions against nature.

That interpretation is wildly inconsistent with the entirety of Scripture, and completely counter to how we've already acknowledged God engages with God's creation.

In his seminal work on sabbath, Rabbi Abraham Heschel describes the violence and harm we do to ourselves and to the creation God commands us to care for when we insist on subduing it. Heschel writes, "To gain control of the world of space is certainly one of our tasks. The danger begins when in gaining power in the realm of space we forfeit all aspirations in the realm of time. There is a realm of time where the goal is not to have but to be, not to own but to give, not to control but to share, not to subdue but to be in accord. Life goes wrong when the control of space, the acquisition of things of space, becomes our sole concern" (3).

In other words, as the writer of Ecclesiastes tells us in chapter 3, "to everything, there is a season." We do great harm when we—in our efforts to eke more production from our earth for our own personal gain—do not allow creation to rest for a season as commanded in Leviticus. We enact violence on our common home when we act as though it is ours to do with as we please rather than cherishing it for what it is—a gift from God.

In *Laudato Si'*, no. 82, Pope Francis writes, "When nature is viewed solely as a source of profit and gain, this has serious consequences for society. This vision of 'might is right' has engendered immense inequality, injustice and acts of violence against the majority of humanity, since resources end up in the hands of the first comer or the most powerful: the winner takes all. Completely at odds with this model are the ideals of harmony, justice, fraternity and peace as proposed by Jesus."

Our lack of care for creation is not simply detrimental to the environment. It is intrinsically linked to the rending of the fabric of our society. This is a tale as old as time. In the 700s BC, the prophet Hosea linked the fate of creation to social justice: "Hear the word of the Lord, O people of Israel, for the Lord has an indictment against the inhabitants of the land. There is no faithfulness or loyalty and no knowledge of God in the land. Swearing, lying, and murder, and stealing and adultery break out; bloodshed follows bloodshed. Therefore the land mourns, and all who live in it languish; together with the wild animals and the birds of the air, even the fish of the sea are perishing" (4:1-3). Our selfishness and greed are not only destructive to ourselves and our communities but ultimately destroy the very place we call home.

The truth is, we are created beings, and like creation itself, we groan and suffer from the abuses we've committed and endured. Our earth is not merely decaying, it is actively, violently being destroyed. It, like we, longs for freedom, peace, and rest.

> **The truth is, we are created beings, and like creation itself, we groan and suffer from the abuses we've committed and endured. Our earth is not merely decaying, it is actively, violently being destroyed. It, like we, longs for freedom, peace, and rest.**

We Can Have Hope

Every day, we are confronted with new, dire statistics about the environment. We see the increase of wildfires, floods, and droughts. We learn of habitats being destroyed. And we wonder what we can do to bring about peace with creation.

We do not have to remain indifferent to the weeping of the earth. We also do not have to throw up our hands in despair. In Romans, Paul doesn't leave us groaning along with creation. He speaks to us of hope!

As people of the resurrection, God makes us able to overcome inevitable decay and death. God is making all things new. It is this hope that fuels us into action. Our awareness of the state of the world produces groaning, yes, but thanks to the hope that we have, that groaning leads to new life! We are called to join in the work to bring justice and peace that the whole of creation yearns for.

Perhaps we begin by naming our concern. What one specific thing needs our attention today? Share that concern with fellow followers of Jesus so that you can pray, hope, and take action together. Remind one another that, as those created in Jesus' image, we work together to make things whole.

Discuss and Act

1. What steps have you personally taken to live at peace with creation? Share with the group if you are comfortable.
2. Can you think of a time when you noticed a group being "labeled" or "named" in such a way that it became easy to marginalize or mistreat them? What actions could you take to counteract those dynamics?
3. As you consider peace with creation, how does Leviticus 25:23 inform your understanding? How does this understanding differ from the reality of the world in which we live? How might things be different if we lived into the truth of God's ownership?

4. Name places where the earth is groaning in agony—places that have experienced devastating natural disasters. Pray together for restoration for the people who inhabit the land but also pray for the land itself.

5. Invite someone from a local organization or national group working on creation care to speak to your cohort or congregation. How might you participate in making peace with creation through the work they are doing? Pray that God would show you what is yours to do.

6. Earth Day is each year on April 22. The Season of Creation, fostered by an ecumenical group aimed at caring for creation, kicks off each September 1 with a day of prayer and runs through October 4. How might you engage with the work they are doing? Their website offers resources. Would holding a prayer vigil at your setting be a possibility?

7. Experts state that one million species could face extinction by 2050. That number is too big to comprehend. How might knowing the names of some of those species impact your feelings on that number? The Green Builders website has suggestions for things you can do in your own yard. Which, if any, of these recommendations could you undertake to care for God's creation?

6. Sabbath as Peace of Jesus

Matthew 6:24-34, 11:28-30; John 14:27

Prepare

1. Find a comfortable position and breathe deeply. As you inhale, pray, "I give you my worries." As you exhale, pray, "So I can find rest." Continue this breath prayer for as long as you need.
2. Read Matthew 11:28-30 slowly a couple of times. What word or phrase catches your attention? How does your body feel as you read Jesus' invitation to come to him for rest? If you experience obstacles to saying "yes" to Jesus' invitation, pray that God will remove them.
3. Look up the lyrics to the hymn "I Surrender All." Read them slowly and make them your prayer each morning this week as an invitation to let the day unfold in Christ's presence and each night to seek release from the cares of the day. Notice as the week progresses how your anxiety decreases, and your sense of peace improves.

Share and Pray

1. Welcome one another. As you are comfortable, share your blessings and burdens from the week. Following each person's offering, pray in unison, "In our sharing, we do not carry this alone."

2. Go around the room and have each person say the word "Stop." After a moment of silence, share any emotions that the word evoked. If God were asking you to stop something for twenty-four hours each week, what would it be? Share if you are comfortable.
3. Can you remember a time when you felt overwhelmed with worry or anxiety, and someone helped you carry that load? How did it feel to turn that over?
4. Identify one thing you could release to accept Jesus' invitation to rest. Is it a schedule commitment? A worry? If you are comfortable, share with the group.
5. Name people or groups in your community carrying heavy burdens (such as refugees, day laborers, or victims of violence). Pray together that God would grant them rest.

Jesus says, "Do not worry about your life." Perhaps those don't seem like the most comforting or even realistic words if you or someone you love has just received a life-threatening diagnosis or are facing the loss of a job or family home.

In fact, depending on the circumstances, those words may even sound trite, compassionless, or cruel. "Trite," "compassionless," and "cruel" aren't typically words we use to describe Jesus, so his statement certainly requires deeper examination.

Do Not Worry

In the Gospels, it's clear that Jesus never calls us to a superficial life, unconcerned about our needs or the needs of our neighbors. He never suggests that we turn a blind eye to suffering. He also never promises that life will be easy.

These six words are not intended to placate us. They also aren't meant to be condescending. Rather, they are an invitation. Jesus says that instead of focusing on worry, which eats away at our spirit and stomach lining, we are to focus instead on our relationship with him. Jesus wants for us something much deeper than surface-level nonchalance, which is shallow and unsustainable. He's calling us to a life in yoked relationship with him . . . a life of peace.

Make no mistake, Jesus knows what it is to worry about his own life. He fell to his knees in the garden of Gethsemane, knowing his earthly life was ending the next day. He told his disciples that his soul was deeply grieved. In his anguish, his sweat fell like drops of blood. No superficial emotion here!

But Jesus found peace through his deep, abiding relationship with God. In his night of deepest despair, he spent hours in communion with God. Jesus knew he could relinquish control and trust God with the outcome. This is the peace of Jesus. And it is this peace that he freely gives to us.

Jesus found peace through his deep, abiding relationship with God. In his night of deepest despair, he spent hours in communion with God. Jesus knew he could trust God with the outcome and relinquish control.

Do This Instead

I appreciate that the text in Matthew 6 is not passive. We're not simply bystanders in our own lives, flailing helplessly as the winds blow us to and fro. Notice that the birds are still in flight. They are still building nests and finding food, using the resources God has provided.

But they aren't building storage sheds to store more than a lifetime supply. An accumulation of wealth and stuff does nothing but provide us with more to worry about. *This* is the worry Jesus calls us to release.

We cannot live without the basic provisions of life, and Jesus freely admits that God knows we need those things. But we don't enjoy the simple pleasures life affords when we endlessly pursue more and more, at any price—harming ourselves, our neighbors, and our planet in the process.

This anxious drive, often grounded in a need for control, frays the fabric of our communal life. Living with this kind of worry fills our lives and our bodies with the darkness of unhealthy competition and greed, blinding us to the light of God's loving justice and peace.

We miss the point if we focus solely on meeting our own needs. As children of God, made in God's image, we are a part of something much larger than this, and this text, found in the Sermon on the Mount, brings that to the forefront.

This passage is not simply about reducing our individual anxiety, although that's a wonderful byproduct. Read in context it's clear that

Jesus is also proclaiming God's justice. Economic anxiety is not just an individual problem—it's a societal problem. Obsessions with gaining wealth and power sacrifice people and the whole of creation.

The rest Jesus offers isn't freedom from all work, rendering us rudderless and purposeless. Instead, he is inviting us to yoke ourselves to his work. Work that is free from oppression and fear. Work that is liberating for all.

Yoked to Jesus

We all experience moments of anxiety. In those times, take a moment to notice the source of your anxiety. Can you identify to what, or to whom, you have yoked (committed or bound) yourself? Jesus invites us out of the grind of self-sufficiency and self-absorption by extending his yoke.

A yoke is a crosspiece, typically made of wood, used to fasten two animals together and then attach them to a plow. The intention is to create a shared burden. Depending on who shares your yoke, this can be a good or a bad experience.

When we say "yes" to Jesus' invitation and accept his yoke, we get to join the work he is already doing, and, perhaps more importantly, work at his pace. We no longer need to pull from our own strength. We can let go of our own agenda. And we can trust that there will be time for rest.

When we say "yes" to Jesus' invitation and accept his yoke, we get to join the work he is already doing, and, perhaps more importantly, work at his pace. We no longer need to pull from our own strength. We can let go of our own agenda. And we can trust that there will be time for rest.

This kind of surrender is a difficult challenge for those of us who yearn for control. We want to believe that we are indispensable. Maybe we even believe that there isn't anyone who could do the job better. This kind of thinking is ultimately an oppressive burden for us to bear. It's one that Jesus invites us to lay down.

Jesus understands that when we place ourselves in a yoke we are in a vulnerable position. We open ourselves up to possible manipulation. Once in a yoke, it can be difficult to get out. And yet, so often, in an effort to relieve our anxiety and heavy loads, we yoke ourselves to abusive or overbearing powers. To empires. To those promising quick fixes. This is precisely why Jesus reminds us that he is humble, gentle, and lowly. Jesus is a trusted partner in our work.

Notice also that Jesus doesn't place the yoke on us. We have the agency to choose to pick it up. And, once we do, we become aware immediately that the load is not evenly distributed. Jesus doesn't ask us to work beyond our capability or capacity. Instead, Jesus does the heavy lifting.

In her book *The Spacious Path*, author Tamara Hill Murphy describes it this way: "In the context of Matthew 11, we're obeying the One who is already shouldering the weight of our lives. We obey with our whole selves out of love and gratitude and, in our obedience, find ourselves at rest" (69).

Once we have truly experienced the gentle yoke of Jesus, we become more aware of the loads others are carrying. It is impossible to surrender to Jesus, receive his grace and mercy, and still want others to remain in bondage to burdensome, oppressive systems.

Freeing Others

Once we have truly experienced the gentle yoke of Jesus, we become more aware of the loads others are carrying. It is impossible to surrender to Jesus, receive his grace and mercy, and still want others to remain in bondage to burdensome, oppressive systems.

In responding to Jesus' invitation to sabbath and peace, we understand that we can only fully receive it when it's available to all. Jesus reminds us that peace and wellbeing do not come from inflicting violence on others. It is only when we yoke ourselves to his work of love and justice that we all will find rest for our souls.

Discuss and Act

1. Our congregation created a Garden of Release to be used by the neighborhood. The garden contains hefty rocks, benches, and a rough-hewn cedar cross. A sign extends the invitation to pick up a rock and name it as a specific weight you carry. After praying for release from this burden, you're invited to leave the rock at the foot of the cross. The sign concludes with the passage from Matthew 11. In what way might you or your congregation extend Christ's sabbath invitation to a neighborhood or world in need?

2. The passage from Matthew 11 lists five invitations: Come to me. Take my yoke. Walk with me. Work with me. Keep company with me. Which of these are you most drawn to? Which are you least drawn to? Why?

3. In John 14:27, Jesus says he gives us his peace. What is "my peace" that Jesus is referring to? How have you experienced it in your times of anxiety?

4. Our society values rugged individualism. Does that make it hard to willingly yoke yourself to someone whose ways are not your ways? Why or why not?

5. As you relinquish worry and control over your own life, might that make it easier to relinquish control (real or imagined) over others? Can you give an example?

6. As you continue to give your worries over to Jesus, what might you do with the extra mental capacity you now have? In other words, with what will you replace your worry? Does that feel like sabbath rest?

7. As you close, take another look at the three prayer practices found in the Prepare section of this lesson. Share your experiences with these practices. As a group, choose one of them to engage in together to wrap up this session.

7. Sabbath as Peace from Distractions

Luke 10:38-42; Amos 8:4-7,11; Deuteronomy 5:15; Mark 10:45

Prepare

1. Light a candle to symbolize that God's restful presence is with you. Spend a few minutes luxuriating in God's presence.
2. Make an appointment to spend a portion of each of the next seven days talking to God. You don't need to follow any prescribed prayer. Simply be intentional about spending time with God.
3. Find a private place, lift your arms above your head with fingers stretched wide, and tell God you need help. Use this posture to stretch you beyond your own understanding. Allow your open hands to model your willingness to receive God's peace. Note how this practice makes you feel.
4. Are you overcommitted or distracted? Ask God to help you order your days in a way that is life-giving. Spend thirty minutes in silence and write down words or images that come to mind as you wait.

Share and Pray

1. Locate three candles. After lighting the first, say, "May the Lord bless us with sabbath joy." After lighting the second, say, "May the Lord bless us with sabbath holiness." After lighting the third, say, "May the Lord bless us with sabbath peace."

2. In China it is considered polite to answer the question, "How are you?" with the answer, "Very busy, thank you." Being busy is equated to being in good health. How might you greet one another this morning in ways that speak of your wholeness, rather than your busyness?

3. Are you comfortable with unstructured days? If not, what fears do you have about unstructured time?

4. In what ways does your productivity impact your sense of worthiness? As you are comfortable sharing, do so with the group. What messages does our culture send about the connection between productivity and worth?

5. When you think about ceasing from some of your activities, what emotions come up? If you are retired, how hard was it to adjust to not working?

6. What activities and hobbies don't fit into your usual week? How could these become sabbath activities to foster rest and relationship with God? With family or neighbors?

7. Spend time in prayer for one another.

The story in Luke 10 is a familiar one, and perhaps one that we don't like very much, if we're being honest. Many of us have been service-oriented "Marthas" all our lives, so this story tweaks our sense of fairness. Most of us believe deeply that acts of service and hospitality demonstrate our love for God and neighbor, so Jesus' criticism of Martha feels personal—and maybe even unwarranted.

Most of us believe deeply that acts of service and hospitality demonstrate our love for God and neighbor, so Jesus' criticism of Martha feels personal—and maybe even unwarranted.

But Jesus' rebuke pales in comparison to the fiery

warnings we read from the prophet Amos. Surely those words don't have anything to do with us! We're not cheating people by charging higher prices for less flour! We're not purchasing slaves to grow our wheat, and we're not demanding their sandals as collateral when they can't pay for our high-priced goods.

We're not the ones eager for the Sabbath to end so that we can get back to work and line our pockets! We're not impatient to get back out there to the things we want to do, the things that meet our needs. Are we?

We're not the ones eager for the Sabbath to end so that we can get back to work and line our pockets! We're not impatient to get back out there to the things we want to do, the things that meet our needs. Are we?

Distraction Creates Distance

In the book of Amos, the beloved children of God cannot wait for the Sabbath to be over so that they can get back to fleecing the poor in pursuit of greater profit. In response, the prophet, as prophets often do, lays bare the sins of the Israelites, telling them that their unbridled greed, pursued at the cost of their relationship with God, will be their ruin.

It's no wonder God is heartbroken. It's no mystery why God is so angry. After all, it was a loving, liberating God who brought the Israelites out of bondage. God doesn't want them to return!

Their own scripture, specifically Deuteronomy 5:15, reminded them that once they had been slaves in Egypt, but God brought them out with a strong hand and an outstretched arm. The verse concludes by explaining that this freedom is why God commanded them to keep the Sabbath day—as a gift of time and refreshment, a time to commune with their Source of life and freedom, a moment to be fully aware of God's loving and sustaining presence—with no distractions.

But instead of appreciating this gift of freedom—instead of celebrating it—they disregarded it and used their freedom to enslave others. In verse 11, Amos warns: "The time is surely coming, says the Lord God, when I will send a famine on the land; not a famine of bread, or a thirst for water, but of hearing the words of the Lord."

In other words, their distraction created a soul-sapping, silencing distance.

Distractions Draw Us Away

In our Gospel story, we hear of another distracted person—one rushing about, perhaps out of hearing range of the Lord.

At first glance, this story may seem unfair. After all, Martha was being obedient to the customs of the day. Women were expected to serve—not to sit as disciples at the foot of the teachers. Only men did that.

As one who seeks to imitate Jesus, surely providing welcome and hospitality reflects his love. After all, in Mark 10:45, Jesus refers to himself as one who came to serve. On many occasions in the Gospels, Jesus calls others to discipleship through service—often sacrificial service. So, what is really going on here?

The answer comes in verse 40. Martha shifts from one providing humble service to one who shatters the boundaries of good hospitality. Notice, first of all, that instead of going directly to Mary with her concern, she went instead to her guest, Jesus, and put him on the spot. This is an act of aggression, no matter how gently she spoke.

In essence, she points out to Jesus that his presence has created an injustice in the workload. She is eager for Mary's "sabbath" to be over so that Mary can get back to work. Martha is suggesting that her type of discipleship, serving, has more value than Mary's form of discipleship, listening and learning, and Martha wants Jesus, her guest, to take her side.

But Jesus refuses. He is aware that both are demonstrating acts of discipleship. The issue is the focus of their discipleship. Notice that Jesus doesn't chastise Martha for being busy. Instead, he points out that Martha is *distracted*.

When we are drawn away by our worries, preoccupations, and lists, and don't make time to connect with the Source that offers peace and a renewal of spirit and energy, we will become resentful and will take it out on others—our friends, our siblings, even our Savior.

That word, distracted, means "drawing away." Her work diverts her attention and draws her away from the object of her hospitality, Jesus. When we are drawn away by our worries, preoccupations, and lists, and don't make time to connect with the Source that offers peace and a renewal of spirit and energy, we will become resentful and will take it out on others—our friends, our siblings, even our Savior.

The text doesn't say it, but I imagine Jesus pulls Martha into an embrace, perhaps patting her back as he repeats her name gently, "Martha, Martha. You are distracted, dear one."

He tells her Mary has chosen the "good" thing—not as a comparison, but as an invitation. Mary is basking in the connection with Jesus—a connection that sustains work and service, a connection that prevents resentment and oppression, a connection that cannot be taken away, a connection that leads to peace.

"Come," Jesus invites. "Notice I am with you in all things. Hear from me."

Freedom from Distractions

The story of Martha and Mary reminds me of the story of Brother Lawrence, a seventeenth-century lay brother in a monastery in Paris. By most standards, his life was completely unremarkable. And yet, contrary to what we might expect, his gentle legacy is remembered, treasured, and captured in the small book *The Practice of the Presence of God*.

In the monastery, he was assigned kitchen work, which he "greatly disliked." At least, at first. He complained that the work distracted him from more spiritual pursuits. But, over time he realized that the best way to commune with God was through ordinary work. He wrote, "It is not necessary to have great things to do. I turn my little omelet in the pan for the love of God" (81).

He would acknowledge God's presence in his work, praying, "Work with me, so that my work might be the very best. Receive as an offering of love both my work and all my affections" (82). Brother Lawrence realized our work happens in the presence of God, not just in the name of God.

God is present. And God is speaking still, inviting us into a deeper, peace-filled relationship. Are we listening? Are we aware of God's presence? Or are we distracted?

As we become less distracted and drawn away, we are less likely to become a stumbling block to another's sabbath. We won't, like the Israelites, insist that others work with no rest. We won't, like Martha, seek to pull our Marys away from the feet of Jesus, but will instead recognize Christ's presence in our own kitchens, too.

As we practice and value sabbath renewal, we will no longer draw others away from their own sabbath practices, and instead, extend the same rest and soul care to everyone we encounter. May it be so.

Discuss and Act

1. When do you most often find yourself worried and distracted? What activities monopolize your attention, drawing you away from God? What steps could you take to find better balance and redirect your attention to the God who offers rest and peace?
2. How do worry and anxiety spill over into your daily living? Does this affect your behavior? Your physical health?
3. Are you someone who always needs to be working hard and accomplishing things? What are the ways you need to slow down and let your soul be fed? What activities are soul-feeding for you?
4. Does your faith community practice and encourage a regular rhythm of rest? Do you have appropriate term limits for lay leaders so that they can step away and renew? Does your congregation encourage and support pastoral sabbath renewal? If not, how can you become more aligned with God's call to rest? How can you champion that for others in your sphere of influence?
5. Are you aware of businesses that don't provide adequate breaks, vacation, sick leave, or family leave to their employees? Do you feel any responsibility to speak against those practices? Why or why not?
6. If you felt the call to address substandard working conditions, unjust labor laws, or inappropriate work-life balance, how might you go about it?
7. Do we expect others to serve us on Sundays or holidays instead of allowing them time with God and their families? What steps could we take to change our approach?

8. Sabbath as Justice and Peace

Exodus 1:11-14, 5:1-19, 20:1-2, 9-10, 35:3; Deuteronomy 5:12-15; Luke 13:10-17

Prepare

1. Light a candle. What happens when you suffocate the flame? Reignite the flame and place your hands around it to protect the flame from the wind. Notice how your hands can either kindle or kill the flame.
2. God self-identifies as a liberator. Spend some time in prayer, offering to God things from which you need liberating. Ask God to reveal any other hidden places of bondage that you need to release.
3. Have you ever heard, or said, some version of this phrase?: "I'll have time to rest when I'm dead." Was it uttered with a sense of pride? A sense of inevitability? How does this phrase make you feel?

Share and Pray

1. Welcome one another. Go around the room, taking turns offering this blessing to each other: "You are made in God's image, so today you shall rest." Does receiving this blessing give you a sense of "permission" to take sabbath today?

2. Offer your joys and concerns for the week. As each person shares, cup your hands to receive what they say. When they finish, raise your cupped hands to the ceiling and say in unison, "We lift this all to God." Repeat as each one shares.

3. Throughout the course of human history there has been struggle around a healthy rhythm of work. For instance, the forty-hour work week was established in the United States only in 1938. In some cultures, each workday includes time for siesta. What feels like a healthy rhythm of work and rest to you? Explain your reasons.

4. Do you feel that modern technology has blurred or even eradicated the boundaries between work and leisure time? Why or why not?

5. Look up the origins of Labor Day. It was established, in part, to address the violence that resulted from oppressive working conditions. How does this fit with what you are learning about sabbath as God's call to peace?

6. We are called human "beings," not human "doings." How might remembering that truth each morning influence your daily schedule?

In Exodus 20:2, the "preamble" to the Ten Commandments, God says, "I am the LORD your God, the one who brought you out of the land of Egypt, out of the house of slavery."

Before God begins to lay out the terms of a new covenant, God reveals who God is—One who liberates! God frees God's people from slavery, and from those who support and benefit from oppressive economic systems. With this single sentence, we learn that God's power and leadership are unlike any we have ever known.

Pharoah's Leadership

In Exodus 5, we learn that Pharoah, the king of Egypt, is arrogant and afraid. These attributes stand in stark contrast to God and are not a strong foundation for effective leadership. We have seen throughout the course of history that leadership rooted in arrogance and fear never produces good decisions or life-giving outcomes. There's a reason why God urgently and continuously implores us to humble ourselves and to fear not!

Pharoah is afraid because the Hebrew slaves outnumber him and his people, potentially making them difficult to control. To mitigate this perceived problem, one of the first things Pharoah does is refuse the Israelites' request for time for worship on the Sabbath. In fact, he erupts at their request, letting his fear boil over into anger, hostility, and ultimately abuse.

Pharoah is afraid because the Hebrew slaves outnumber him and his people, potentially making them difficult to control. To mitigate this perceived problem, one of the first things Pharoah does is refuse the Israelites' request for time for worship on the Sabbath.

We hear it in the language of this text. In the first lesson of this study, we considered the rhythm of rest found in Genesis 1. It was soothing, almost like a lullaby. There is a rhythm to this passage as well—but it is most certainly not restful.

Get to work!
You may not stop working!
Go and gather your own straw!
Make the same number of bricks!
Assign heavier work!
I will not give you straw!
Go and get straw yourself!
Complete your work!
Finish the assignment!
Make bricks!
You are lazy, lazy!
Go now and work!
No straw will be provided!
Make the same number of bricks!
You must make the same number of bricks!

Can you hear it? It's like an anvil pounding and pounding. The words themselves are as relentless as the work they require. Into this cacophonous system, Moses and Aaron proclaim, "Let my people go."

Oppression!

We hear the voices of a lot of characters in this passage: Moses and Aaron, Pharaoh, the Egyptian taskmasters, and the Hebrew supervisors. But lest we forget, there is another group of characters mentioned here. One whose voices we never hear. The Hebrew slaves are very present, but they are never permitted to speak.

Pharaoh kept them so busy they had no time to speak up for themselves. They had no time to listen either. The constant pressure for productivity muted not only their voices, but also the voice of God calling them to another way of peaceful, restful living.

Pharaoh kept them so busy they had no time to speak up for themselves. They had no time to listen either. The constant pressure for productivity muted not only their voices, but also the voice of God calling them to another way of peaceful, restful living.

We know this was Pharaoh's intent because he said it out loud in verse 9: "Keep them busy so that they can't listen to the lure of Sabbath rest" (author's translation). In other words: If they are well-rested, they can work together to overthrow my reign!

And what a reign of terror it was. In a schedule like this, there was clearly no sabbath for the slaves. But there was also no sabbath for the supervisors and taskmasters who were forced to oversee this abusive schedule. And, ultimately, because of his constant fear and anger, there was no sabbath, no peace, for Pharaoh either.

Finally, the Israelite supervisors spoke up, crying out to Pharaoh, calling him "unjust." Not brutal, though he was. Not cruel. Unjust.

What bravery it must have taken to speak out against the injustice of this brutal regime. Bravery that resulted in extreme suffering. This abusive ruler had them beaten because of their demands.

But here's the good news. And it's very good news. Our God will not let the unjust reign forever. God calls God's people to be a part of the liberation. Moses and Aaron, the Hebrew supervisors . . . and us.

Liberation!

As I've researched this topic of sabbath, I've worked hard at, and benefitted from, my own new sabbath practices. As I've created new habits, I've internalized how crucial they are to my physical, mental, and spiritual well-being. These new practices have reduced the violence I've committed to my own body, to my community, and to my family, caused in part by my lack of availability. I've become aware of my over-functioning, and I want to do better. For myself. And for others.

Especially for others.

In conversations with many people surrounding the topic of sabbath, I've heard from "the voiceless," those on the margins, those who feel they can't take a day of rest—even a moment of rest—because they are working multiple jobs simply trying to make ends meet. This is not sustainable, and it's clearly not biblical.

Author Tamara Hill Murphy invites us into the idea of "spacious work." She writes, "Saying yes to spacious work will help us feel more keenly the injustices of forced and underpaid labor and will help us notice the dignity of the essential workers in our society. We will prayerfully work for laws and economies that allow everyone to work as the beloved imago Dei [image of God]" (144).

Theologian Walter Brueggemann agrees, writing that today, systems that oppress and exploit workers are so much a part of the way of life that we hardly notice. Abuse has been normalized. Exhaustion is the rule, not the exception. "Anxiety is a given, and violence is unexamined as the 'cost of doing business'" (17).

Into this system, Moses and Aaron proclaimed, "Let my people go." Into this system, we are also called to lift our voices and demand justice. Demand change.

Jesus Liberates!

In Luke 13, we find a story of Jesus breaking the Sabbath rule. This story has several similarities with the one found in Exodus. First, notice that the nameless, marginalized woman doesn't ask for anything. She doesn't approach Jesus, and she doesn't express her need. Perhaps after eighteen years she is used to being unseen. Like the Israelite slaves, she is voiceless, and she is in bondage.

But Jesus sees her. He sees her and releases her from bondage . . . on the Sabbath. Which, contrary to what the leader of the synagogue insisted, is actually a purpose of the Sabbath.

Deuteronomy 5:15 says, "Remember that you were a slave in the land of Egypt, and the Lord your God brought you out from there with a mighty hand and an outstretched arm; *therefore*, the Lord your God commanded you to keep the Sabbath day" (emphasis added).

The leader of the synagogue who sought to protect the Sabbath forgot its link to liberation. He forgot that the Sabbath and the synagogue were not the only holy and precious things. The woman was also holy—also worthy.

A further similarity between these passages is a willingness to speak truth and justice to power. Jesus confronts the leader of the synagogue just as Moses and Aaron confronted Pharoah. Jesus challenges his followers to do the same, no matter our comfort level with confrontation. Systems of oppression must be opposed.

Aligning ourselves with Jesus the liberator provides us with tremendous blessings as well. We experience moments of outrageous beauty as a result. We bear witness to the joy that liberation brings. Having been freed from her bondage, this voiceless woman regains her voice. She opens her mouth and sings out in praise, fully engaging, as her Creator intended, in life-giving, peace-making, Sabbath worship!

Aligning ourselves with Jesus the liberator provides us with tremendous blessings as well. We experience moments of outrageous beauty as a result. We bear witness to the joy that liberation brings. Having been freed from her bondage, this voiceless woman regains her voice. She opens her mouth and sings out in praise, fully engaging, as her Creator intended, in life-giving, peace-making, Sabbath worship!

For this reason, do not be afraid at the work ahead of us—the work God is calling us to—described in the words penned by poet and lyricist Miriam Therese Winter:

"Surely / You meant / when You lifted / her up / Long ago / To your praise, / Compassionate One, / not one woman / only / but all women, / bent, / by unbending ways" (https://re-worship.blogspot.com/2013/07/gospel-reflection-luke-13-10-17.html).

Discuss and Act

1. At the heart of the Civil Rights movement, the following questions were raised and continue to be relevant today. As people of God, should we obey human laws that marginalize, oppress, or dehumanize people? What should we do when confronted with unjust laws that contradict the commandments of God? How would you answer these questions today?

2. In God's kin-dom, the path to peace "is not the absence of conflict, but the holy disruption of laws and practices that prevent all humanity from realizing its full and authentic identity as 'children of God'" (Simpson 62). What does "holy disruption" look like to you? Pray about where God might be calling you to participate in holy disruption.
3. What is one step you could take to release yourself or others from the Pharoah's productivity trap?
4. In the 1800s, abolitionists called out the hypocrisy of Christian slaveholders who broke God's Sabbath command by forcing slaves to work on Sundays. They offered this as a reason to end the system of slavery. Do these types of labor practices still exist in American culture today? If so, how might you be called to address it?
5. In Genesis 47, we're told Pharoah required so much production from the slaves that even more bricks were needed to build more storage facilities. Consider how many storage facilities are in your local community. If we had less "need" for those facilities, how might that land be repurposed? Affordable housing? Green space?
6. God worked six days to bring the world into existence and then rested. When we refuse to participate in a regular rhythm of rest, we are patterning our lives on something other than God. We are, in fact, more like Pharoah. How does that understanding impact your commitment to practice sabbath-keeping? How does it inspire you to work for sabbath for others?

9. Sabbath as Peace and Freedom

1 Samuel 21:1-6; Micah 6:3-8; Mark 2:23–3:6; Matthew 12:7

Prepare

1. Light a battery-operated tea light, then hide it between your hands so that you cannot see the light. As you inhale, pray, "God, give me freedom." As you exhale, pray, "to let your light shine." Repeat this breath prayer several times. Slowly open your hands to reveal the light.
2. Are there obligations or rules in your life that make you feel stuck? What would it take to free yourself from those feelings? Would something be lost if those obligations or rules were removed from your life? Spend time in prayer asking God for wisdom and discernment.
3. In what ways do you find comfort in rules and laws? Have you ever felt that following rules helped you earn God's love? If so, how? Have you felt that following rules nurtured your relationship with God and with others? If so, how?

Share and Pray

1. Welcome one another by sharing a rule your parents had that you

found unfair, arbitrary, or just silly. Looking back, can you understand why this rule existed?

2. Share prayer concerns around the circle, giving grace for those who do not wish to share. As each person finishes, say in unison, "Listening God, hear your children's prayers."

3. As your group has gathered around this study, have you noticed any unspoken rules forming? If so, name them. For instance, do you sit in the same place each week? Is there one person who always shares first?

4. Have you ever been in a situation where you, or someone else, did something outside the "rules"—written or otherwise? How did that feel? How was the situation addressed or resolved?

5. What freedom do we have to break rules? Are there rules that must never be broken? If so, what are they?

6. What rules should be included (or not) in our sabbath practices? How do the rules for observances of the Sabbath in Jesus' time and the rules for sabbath observance in modern times relate (or not) to each other?

In 1708, eight men and women gathered in their homes in Germany to pore over scripture together, seeking guidance from the Holy Spirit for an obedient way to live out their faith. After a significant time of prayer, study, and conversation, they made the decision to be re-baptized as adults, which went against their own faith tradition and the law.

What followed that decision was a season of growth, but also a series of persecutions that left many threatened, injured, bankrupt, or in jail. It ultimately resulted in an exodus to colonial America.

Breaking rules when compelled by faith and facing backlash for that transgression—truly, there is nothing new under the sun.

Jesus Breaks Sabbath Rules

The author of the Gospel of Mark recounts an episode in which Jesus broke Sabbath rules, not once, but twice. The first instance seems innocent enough. Jesus and his disciples were walking and apparently worked up an appetite. This could have been due to poor planning. Maybe they didn't know how long the journey would take. Perhaps they hadn't prepared and packed enough food. Regardless of the reason, their physical needs were met when they gleaned some wheat from a field as they passed.

However, this action was an infraction of Sabbath rules and caught the attention of some Pharisees who were quick to point it out to Jesus. He responded in a very "Jesus way" by referring back to Scripture—their shared, common Scripture. Jesus noted that King David had done something similar (although one could argue, much worse!) when he and his men were hungry on the Sabbath. In that story, recorded in 1 Samuel 21, David told the priest he was carrying out a mission from God. In highlighting this story, was Jesus saying the same was true for himself?

Jesus made a bold, direct claim: The Sabbath was created for humans, not the other way around.

Jesus then made a bold, direct claim: The Sabbath was created for humans, not the other way around. The rules cannot and do not box in the Son of man and his purpose.

The Confrontation Continues

Seemingly on the same day, Jesus entered the synagogue and offered an opportunity for a do-over. Even knowing the hard-heartedness of those who opposed him, he provided another chance for their change of heart. Realizing the Pharisees were eager to catch him in another Sabbath violation, Jesus called forward a man who suffered from a withered hand. He asked those watching, "Is it lawful to do good or to do harm on the Sabbath, to save life or to kill?" (Mark 3:4).

I'm intrigued by this question. Neither of the Sabbath-breaking situations were life-threatening. The disciples wouldn't have been vanquished by hunger in the few remaining hours before sundown. And the man could have just as easily waited a few more hours for healing. In fact, having his hand restored on the Sabbath didn't allow him to return to work in the immediate aftermath anyway, as he also had Sabbath rules to follow.

Did Jesus even commit a violation when he provided healing? He didn't touch the man. He didn't make a salve from mud and place it on the man's hand. He simply spoke healing into being. Was speaking also against Sabbath rules?

Further, did Jesus even commit a violation when he provided healing? He didn't touch the man. He didn't make a salve from mud and place it on the man's hand. He simply spoke healing into being. Was speaking also against Sabbath rules? Or did that demonstration of spoken, healing power align Jesus even more closely with the God who spoke life into being?

Who Was Being Healed?

The man with the withered hand was certainly healed. But Jesus offered a different kind of healing to all who witnessed this encounter. This group of Pharisees had forgotten the purpose of the Sabbath: to rest alongside a God who rests, and to liberate those in bondage. They had become slaves to the rules, and enslavers of those within their sphere of control.

It was to these Pharisees that Jesus said, "If you had known what this means, 'I desire mercy and not sacrifice,' you would not have condemned the guiltless" (Matthew 12:7). Their strict adherence to the rules had blinded them to the compassion and mercy they needed to extend. Jesus grieved their stubborn hearts and yearned for their healing, too.

Freedom from Legalism

Not everyone subscribed to these strict, unbending rules. Heschel writes, "The ancient rabbis knew that excessive piety may endanger the fulfilment of the essence of the law. There is nothing more important, according to the Torah, than to preserve human life . . . Even when there is the slightest possibility that a life may be at stake one may disregard every prohibition of the law (except idolatry, adultery, and murder). One must sacrifice mitzvot *for the sake of man* rather than sacrifice man *for the sake of mitzvot*" (Heschel, 17).

Legalism without compassion often breeds harm and conflict. Barbara Brown Taylor mused about what happens when people try to solve conflicts simply by launching Bible verses at one another. In her book *Leaving Church*, she writes: "I can begin to love the dried ink marks more than the encounters that gave rise to them. If I am not careful, I can decide that I am really much happier reading my Bible than I am entering into what God is doing in my own time and place. . . . The whole purpose of the Bible, it seems to me, is to convince people to set the written words down in order to become living words in the world for God's sake" (107).

Jesus cautions us that, when presented with an opportunity to extend a healing hand, we must not neglect to act, claiming that God's sabbath somehow prevents such works of compassion. Jesus didn't keep the Sabbath rules for self-preservation, and he didn't break the rules to help himself either. He broke the Sabbath rules to align himself more closely with the God who heals and frees people from bondage.

Jesus challenges us to find the deeper justice expressed in the law and to act on it. Moment by moment, we are encouraged to look at time-honored traditions and familiar rules through the lenses of compassion, justice, and peace. Have we allowed the worship of our heritage and our rules to blind us to our neighbors' needs? Have we become hard-hearted and indifferent to Christ's presence on the margins?

Jesus challenges us to find the deeper justice expressed in the law and to act on it. Moment by moment, we are encouraged to look at time-honored traditions and familiar rules through the lenses of compassion, justice, and peace. Have we allowed the worship of our heritage and our rules to blind us to our neighbors' needs? Have we become hard-hearted and indifferent to Christ's presence on the margins?

Through the prophet Micah, God reminds the Israelites once again of God's liberating freedom. God is the one who brought the people out of the house of slavery in Egypt. God doesn't want their response to this gift to be a re-entry into slavery. Set aside the rules surrounding burnt offerings and sacrifices, God says, and do what is good. Do justice. Love kindness. And walk—take action—humbly with God.

We don't practice sabbath to honor the rules. We practice sabbath to enter a deeper awareness of what Jesus is doing in our midst. We see with Jesus' eyes. And we join Jesus in his ministry of healing and justice.

As we abide with the one who brings healing, justice, and wholeness, our own brokenness, our own need for healing, is lovingly cared for in those moments. Through the freedom of sabbath, Jesus provides justice and peace for us, our family of faith, and the world.

Discuss and Act

1. Having read the passages from 1 Samuel and Mark, what similarities and differences do you note?

2. As you read these passages, who is in violation of the Sabbath—the one who follows the spirit of the law, or the one follows the letter of the law? Which of these brings us closer to the heart of God? How does this understanding fit with Jesus' words in Mark 2:27?

3. Consider how the following questions might provide clarity and/or freedom around rules: For whom is the rule being broken? Does the broken rule benefit us and improve our own power or status, or is the rule being broken to serve those in need? Does breaking the rule free up something that has become rigid over time?

4. Some congregations practice "Fifth Sundays," when instead of meeting in their church buildings, they go out into their communities to meet the needs of their neighbors as an act of sabbath worship. How might that idea be received by your faith community? What other ways to promote sabbath renewal in your faith setting or neighborhood might break with tradition but meet a real need? Choose one of these ideas to engage in as a group.

5. This lesson begins with the story of the birth of the Church of the Brethren. Their story echoes the birth of the Anabaptist tradition as well. Can you think of other examples where people followed their perceived call to serve God and their neighbors, even when it violated the norms and the rules of their faith community? Have you ever had an experience like that?

10.

Sabbath as Peace with Neighbors

Genesis 2:18; Exodus 20:17; Mark 12:28-34; Luke 12:13-21; Acts 9:1-19; Romans 13:9; Philippians 4:11-13

Prepare

1. Sit in a comfortable chair. Close your eyes and lay your palms open, face up, in your lap. As you breathe, invite God to remove the desire to clutch on to possessions too tightly. Ask God to fill you instead with peace.

2. Read Genesis 2:18. God's intention is for us to live in community. Isolation and loneliness lead to restlessness—a lack of peace. Take a moment to identify a relationship in your life that leaves you feeling accepted, joyful, and peaceful. Make an appointment for a phone call or an in-person visit. Notice how time spent with that person restores your soul.

3. Sit back and watch people walk by. Or look in your church directory. As you look at each face or put your finger over each name, pray: "May you have enough. May you be at peace." Notice how you feel after offering this blessing over and over.

Share and Pray

1. As you gather, take turns looking at the person to your right and offering this blessing, "May you have enough. May you be at peace." Once each individual has been blessed, share this prayer in unison: "May all our neighbors have enough. May all our neighbors be at peace."
2. Share joys and concerns from the week, respecting those who choose not to share. Pray together with gratitude over the needs expressed.
3. Read, sing, or listen to the hymn "Take Time to Be Holy." Share with the group your vision of what it means to "take time to be holy."
4. Share with the group a time when you were in need, and God answered your prayer for help through the generosity of another person. Or share a time when you were an answer to prayer, having shared from your abundance with someone in need. Did these experiences draw you closer to God and to your neighbor? Explain.
5. Read Exodus 20:17. Before looking in a dictionary, define the word "covet" in your own words. Is it a thought or desire? Does it require action to make it a sin?
6. After creating your own definition, look up the word "covet" in a dictionary. Does the definition suggest that an action must accompany a desire in order for a thought to be considered coveting? Why or why not?

Very early in my Christian formation, I learned the words, "Thou shall not covet." While I wasn't sure exactly what coveting was, I knew it was bad! And so, it surprised me when, a few years later, a man I believed to be a great person of faith told me he would covet my prayers. Did that mean he was jealous of my prayers? Did that mean he would somehow take my prayers from me?

Those thoughts were scary and violating to my young self. They were also, thankfully, not quite right.

Beloved Community

Jesus tells us in Mark 12:29-31 that the greatest commandment is to love God with all our heart, being, mind, and strength, and the second greatest command is to love our neighbor as ourselves.

While we may struggle with the question of who exactly is our neighbor, scripture is clear about how we are to love them. Romans 13:9 specifically reiterates four of the Ten Commandments, "You shall not commit adultery; you shall not murder; you shall not steal; you shall not covet," revealing that they are the process through which we love our neighbors as ourselves. Through the Ten Commandments, God invites us to become God's friend, and to live in harmony with our neighbors.

While we may struggle with the question of who exactly is our neighbor, scripture is clear about how we are to love them. Romans 13:9 specifically reiterates four of the Ten Commandments, "You shall not commit adultery; you shall not murder; you shall not steal; you shall not covet," revealing that they are the process through which we love our neighbors as ourselves.

Refraining from coveting (Exodus 20:17, the tenth commandment) is, perhaps surprisingly, the most crucial component in creating the beloved community. Of all the commandments, only this one is repeated: "Thou shall not covet . . . Thou shall not covet." This repetition stresses its significant importance.

In fact, the tenth commandment to refrain from coveting is so important in maintaining neighborly relationships that the word "neighbor" is mentioned three times in the verse. To keep from coveting, we are to follow the golden rule, respecting our neighbors and our neighbors' things, the way we wish to be respected.

What's the Harm?

Walter Brueggemann offers context for the word "covet" in the biblical tradition, stating that it includes both a *desire* and an *action*. Perhaps that's what distinguishes it from stealing. Even yearning for something someone else has harms us. It creates within us a deep dissatisfaction—an unhealthy awareness of the things we believe we lack rather than a focus on the blessings we have. Coveting fosters an anxiety that we will never have enough. There is no peace in that.

Taking action on the desire to have what others have is devastating to the community. It is an act of violence to take what belongs to someone else. We injure not only our communities, but also ourselves, by our need to accumulate more and more. This unhealthy competition and comparison with our neighbors to have the best and most "stuff," and to restlessly and recklessly seek to get ahead at all costs, destroys any possibility of community. This is true in our one-on-one relationships, and in our broader community relationships, too.

The Antidote

Practicing sabbath is an invitation to step away from the need for accumulation. It provides a space to relieve the anxiety of never having enough—an anxiety that often propels us to violent actions that diminish community. When we say "yes" to the practice of sabbath, we say "no" to the worship and pursuit of things that do not ultimately satisfy, things that do not fill us with peace.

Practicing sabbath doesn't mean that we divest of all our possessions. It doesn't mean that we withdraw from society. Instead, sabbath's practices of relationship and rest free us from becoming a slave to stuff. Sabbath releases us from the anxiety of accumulation. It helps us hold the contradiction of having things, yet also being able to live without them.

Practicing sabbath is an invitation to step away from the need for accumulation. It provides a space to relieve the anxiety of never having enough—an anxiety that often propels us to violent actions that diminish community. When we say "yes" to the practice of sabbath, we say "no" to the worship and pursuit of things that do not ultimately satisfy, things that do not fill us with peace.

Love God and Love Your Neighbor

Love God and love your neighbor are the greatest commands. They are the commands that bookend the Ten Commandments. The first commandment insists that we have no other god than our God. Following this command preserves relationship with God by casting out idolatry. The last commandment, to refrain from coveting, preserves our relationship with our neighbors by casting out greed.

The first commandment insists that we have no other god than our God. Following this command preserves relationship with God by casting out idolatry. The last commandment, to refrain from coveting, preserves our relationship with our neighbors by casting out greed.

Jesus warns about the harmful effects that greed has on relationships, in the Gospel of Luke. In this account, Jesus is approached by a person in the crowd insisting that Jesus intervene on his behalf. He demands a portion of the family inheritance. In this story, the person covets what his brother has.

It's possible that this is a legitimate request. It could be that the person in the crowd has been denied his fair share of the family legacy by an older brother who was keeping more than the two-thirds inheritance to which he was entitled. However, the details aren't spelled out, and Jesus' response makes me wonder.

Jesus is not eager to get involved in a family feud, but he is also not one to miss a teachable moment, and so he cautions against greed. He warns against putting too much stock in the accumulation of possessions. He admonishes against a closed fist that refuses to share.

Jesus then tells a parable of a rich landowner with a big problem. His land produced so much grain that he couldn't consume it all. To solve his problem, he decides to build more barns. In his decision-making process, he consults *himself* only: "And he thought to himself, 'What should I do, for I have no place to store my crops?'" (Luke 12:17). At no time does he consult God, offer thanks to God, or consider the possibility of sharing with his community.

At no time does he consider whether he has enough.

This parable invites us all to reflect thoughtfully on what we want and why we want it. What constitutes "enough?"

Contentment Leads to Peace

Perhaps the best example of a life dramatically altered by God's call to peace is found in Acts 9. As we read, we find that Saul's life was changed in more ways than just his name. He was once a person filled with ambition to succeed at all costs—condoning and committing heinous acts of violence against his neighbors to prove his righteousness and commitment to God.

God's response was to sideline him, striking him blind. Our bodies do that to us sometimes. A lack of appropriate sabbath rest can lead to strokes and heart attacks, forcing us to reexamine our priorities.

Paul spent three years listening to and abiding with God, and was entirely transformed by this precious time dwelling in the heart of God. As he grew to understand God's will, his priorities aligned with God's, helping him build up communities rather than destroy them.

Much later, Paul, from a prison cell, described his life-altering change in Philippians 4:12-13 (CEB), saying: "I have learned the secret to being content in any and every circumstance . . . I can endure all these things through the power of the one who gives me strength."

No one would covet Paul's final living conditions. No one would want to change places with him. However, Paul thrived. Through intentional and regular time spent basking in God's presence, partaking of God's sabbath, Paul was content. He had enough. And he could live in peace with everyone, regardless of his circumstances. May all God's people do the same.

Discuss and Act

1. Read, sing, or listen again to the hymn "Take Time to Be Holy." How might this hymn summarize this Bible study and encourage the practice of newly formed sabbath habits?

2. What does it mean to be rich towards God? How might that counteract the temptation to covet?

3. In the Prepare section of Session 2, you were invited to rewrite the commandment to abstain from coveting in a positive manner. Following this lesson, would you revise your work? If so, how?

4. What would you like your legacy to be? When people remember you, would you like them to say, "He sure spent a lot of time at the office"? Or, "She always had the most fashionable clothing"? Or, "He loved God, his family, and his neighbors, and he demonstrated that through (fill in the blank)"? Share your hopes for your legacy. What steps might you take to move in that direction, with God's help?

5. To begin this session, you prayed, "May all our neighbors have enough. May all our neighbors be at peace." What actions can you

take to ensure that your neighbors have enough: Participate in a food drive? Work with nonprofits and government agencies to seek adequate, affordable housing? Something else? Agree on one idea you can do together and take steps to enact it.

6. Apply what you've learned from other sessions. How are we to care for the earth's bounty? How are we to focus on our relationship with God instead of creating the idol of self-sufficiency and productivity? How can we say with conviction, "We have enough, and we are at peace"?

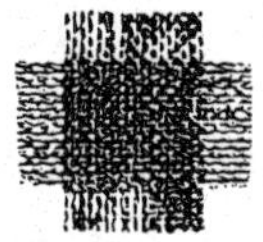

Bibliography

Berry, Wendell. *A Timbered Choir: The Sabbath Poems 1979-1997.* New York: Counterpoint, 1998.

Brother Lawrence. *The Practice of the Presence of God.* New Kensington, PA: Whitaker House, 1982.

Brueggemann, Walter. *Sabbath as Resistance: Saying No to the Culture of Now*. Louisville, KY: Westminster John Knox Press, 2017.

Dalton-Smith, M.D., Saundra. *Sacred Rest: Recover your Life, Renew your Energy, Restore your Sanity*. New York: FaithWords, 2017.

"Eugene Peterson on Being a Real Pastor." *Relevant*, June 7, 2011. https://relevantmagazine.com/life5/1262-eugene-peterson-on-being-a-real-pastor/.

Friedman, Gillian. "Poll: Are the Ten Commandments still relevant today? Americans and Brits differ, and millennials stand out." *Deseret News*, March 28, 2018. https://www.deseret.com/2018/3/28/20642391/poll-are-the-ten-commandments-still-relevant-today-americans-and-brits-differ-and-millennials-stand/.

Heschel, Abraham Joshua. *The Sabbath.* New York: Farrar, Straus, Giroux, 2005.

Muller, Wayne. *Sabbath: Finding Rest, Renewal, and Delight in our Busy Lives.* New York: Bantam, 2000.

Murphy, Tamara Hill. *The Spacious Path: Practicing the Restful Way of Jesus in a Fragmented World*. Harrisonburg, VA: Herald Press, 2023.

Riess, Jana. *Flunking Sainthood: A Year of Breaking the Sabbath, Forgetting to Pray, and Still Loving My Neighbor*. Brewster, MA: Paraclete Press, 2011.

Simpson, Gary V. *Connections*. Year B vol. 2. Louisville, KY: Westminster John Knox Press, 2020.

Taylor, Barbara Brown. *An Altar in the World: A Geography of Faith*. New York: HarperOne, 2009.

Warren, Tish Harrison. *Liturgy of the Ordinary: Sacred Practices in Everyday Life*. Downers Grove, IL: IVP Books, 2016.